Leaning West

Michael C. Keith

Červená Barva Press
Somerville, Massachusetts

Červená Barva Press
P.O. Box 440357
W. Somerville, MA 02144-3222

www.cervenabarvapress.com

Bookstore: www.thelostbookshelf.com

Cover Art: Susanne Riette

Cover Design: William J. Kelle

ISBN: 978-1-950063-28-4

ACKNOWLEDGMENTS

A handful of the pieces in this volume first appeared in the following collections: *The Late Epiphany of a Low-Key Oracle* (Nixes Mate, 2020), *Pieces of Bones and Rags* (Cabal Books, 2021), and *Insomnia 11* (MadHat Press, 2020).

A note of appreciation is owed Michael Brown for helping assure the accuracy of certain terminology as well as references to specific names and locations.

TABLE OF CONTENTS

Leaning West

Devil's Tower

The whistle of the BNSF freight moving on the outskirts of Newcastle, Wyoming, deepens his loneliness. He curses his decision to rent a room in the Stardust Motel. What did he expect for nineteen dollars a night, he thinks, pressing his palms to his ears.

Fearless Youth

Invention is the talent of youth, as judgement is of old age
—Jonathan Swift

Eighty-six-year-old sheep rancher Dollie Brown went off in her own direction after she parked her dented and dusty SUV at the base of a ridge in the Powder River Basin. My two friends (her son and daughter-in-law) and I headed up the rise to gather interesting rock specimens for our respective collections. A half-hour later, our pockets bulging, we walked back down to where the car was parked. In the distance, I spotted Dollie walking toward us. I picked up my pace to meet up with her to see where she'd been and why she'd gone her own way. "Went back to a big critter hole I saw couple weeks ago and stuck a stick down it this time. Then thought that wasn't smart, because something mean could be down there and not take to my poking around its den," she reported. In the few remaining steps back to her aging four-wheel drive, she added, "When I was 70, I'd have kept sticking that hole."

On Bypassing Topeka

"What if on our way to Albuquerque we had driven past
the capital of Kansas and not met Ray Givens at Bobo's
Drive In who turned out to be a perfect match for the
organ that was failing you?"

Bushnell, Nebraska, 1953

The joys of fathers are secret, and so are their grieves and fears.
—Francis Bacon

Our house was at the far edge of town on a dirt road that came to an end at the creek we spent most of every summer fishing. Because we hardly ever caught anything in it, it didn't attract other folks. That was fine with Pa, because he couldn't abide strangers or even people he knew, for that matter. In fact, it seemed he just barely tolerated us, although Ma treated him like he was the nicest person there was. It's not that he wasn't okay with me and my younger brother. It's just that he never stopped telling us he had hidden a gun somewhere close by and he knew how to use it. He would say that out of the blue when we sat with him on the porch or work the fields with him. Blurt it out like there was someone else there with us. It didn't seem like it was intended for us, but it didn't seem like it wasn't. My little brother would ask me about it, but I didn't have an explanation. Finally, we just accepted there was a gun hidden somewhere on the property, and it was important to Pa that we knew it.

Paradise Lost 2

This is his third time to his northern Wyoming friend's 20,000-acre former sheep ranch. Located on the lowlands running up to the snowcapped Big Horn Mountains, its beauty and solitude fill him with a sense of joy and wonder he's experienced nowhere else. *It's such a spiritual place . . . transcendent,* he thinks. This trip he decides to visit the spread on his own a day ahead of checking in with his friend in Sheridan. After previous visits to the sprawling range, he feels confident he can navigate its twisting dirt roads, rocky basins, and jagged rises. Two days later he knows he's made a miscalculation. Out of gas and beyond the reach of a cellphone signal, he begins to think he may never see civilization again. "Goddamn hellhole!!" he howls, making his presence known to a mountain lion just behind the ridge he approaches.

The Compassion of Geography

Follow your bliss . . .

—Joseph Campbell

Somewhere just beyond South Platte, Nebraska, I came alive. I'd been deeply dug into a depression for days now, but when the landscape began to take on the look of the old west I'd seen in countless cowboy movies as a kid, I felt the dark clouds pull away and my gloom lift. "Thank you!" I shouted, from the Silverado window.

Looking for America

Back in the 80s, Craig and his new wife traveled west on their honeymoon. He'd just read Dee Brown's *Bury My Heart at Wounded Knee* and wanted to take the opportunity to visit the site where the subject of the book unfolds. The young couple drove from the northern part of the Pine Ridge Indian Reservation that reaches to Interstate 90 and after two dusty hours on a gravel road came upon the place where 300 Lakota Sioux, mostly women and children, were massacred by the U.S. Cavalry. Expecting to encounter a shiny tourist pavilion like the one they'd just seen at Mt. Rushmore, they were surprised to find a rusty lean-to, crumbling shed, and graffitied historical marker that told of the slaughter in broken English. They were indignant that something more fitting hadn't been erected by the government to commemorate such a tragic event in American history. When they asked a passing tribal elder about it, he replied, "Would Jews have let Hitler build them a shrine?"

The Power of Film

I had no illusions about my films., nor did I consider myself anything special.

–Gene Autry

Allen Halper wanted to be a cowboy since growing up in Queens, New York. He'd spent endless hours in smoky movie houses watching westerns, and he thought the cowboy's life the most wonderful and exciting of anything an adult could do. He did not want to join his father's hosiery manufacturing company, nor did he want to waste his time going to the business college his father attended. So, upon graduating high school, he packed his suitcase, emptied his savings account, and set out for the west, where he planned to look for a job as a ranch hand. He targeted Oakley, Kansas, as a good place to start his search for no other reason than it had been a scene location for a cattle drive in a movie starring Randolph Scott. He figured someone in town could tell him who was hiring. After downing a burger at The Bluff, he made his inquiry and was told the Circle K off Service Road 31 was looking for experienced help. He took a local conveyance to the site and was hired on the spot after telling the foreman he'd been "punching cows" since he was 12. In no time at all he was able to mount a horse.

Red Skins

She saw her first Native American in a country and western bar in Cody, Wyoming, while on a road trip to Yellowstone and was very excited. He wasn't exactly like the Indians in movies or on TV. She'd seen his shirt at Macy's when shopping for a birthday gift for her husband. *I suppose that makes sense these days*, she told herself. Still, it detracted from her image of what indigenous people should look like.

WYO 287

I'm taking a motorcycle ride north from Laramie. It's still chilly even though it's early June. The winds are really whipping across Como Bluff as I near the "world's oldest building"—according to Ripley's *Believe It or Not.* It's made of dinosaur bones, so I guess there's some truth to the claim. It used to be a tourist stop that sold artifacts, namely fossils unearthed in the area. I'm disappointed to discover it's closed, since the main reason I've made the trip up is to buy another chunk of dinosaur musculoskeletal needed to complete a set of bookends. There's an adjacent structure on the buffeted property, and it's deserted as well. For a time, I peruse the site wondering why such a unique place would be abandoned. Sad, I think, returning to the building that was the store. When I peer through one of its dust-covered windows, I can just make out the pelvis of a Stegosaurus.

Child Welfare

Deep down below the surface . . . a small voice says to us, something is out of tune.

—Carl Jung

Mark believed Blake, Nebraska, was a fine place to raise a nine-year-old, even if there was just him to do it—his wife had inexplicably vanished weeks before. There was no crime to speak of in the farming community, so a kid could wander all over without being in any particular danger. Of course, that was before he learned it had been declared the landing site for hostile aliens. When he got the news, it was too late for him to do much about it, except direct his son to go play outside, distracting the invaders enough to allow him time to hide in the storm cellar. It was there he found his missing wife.

Any Day You Can Solve a Mystery Is a Good Day

He found deep rutted wagon wheel tracks against a large boulder at the far edge of his 730-acre spread on the eastern plains of Wyoming. He'd bought the place just three months earlier and was still exploring parts of the property. This particular discovery intrigued him, because it looked as if the impressions came directly out from under the giant rock. *Impossible. How could that be?* he wondered. Upon further inspection, he noticed a set of tracks led up to the other side of the monolith. It was if the wagon had somehow burrowed under the rock and resurfaced on the other side. Or weirder still, had gone through it. Try as he might, he could not come up with a reasonable explanation. He did, however, determine why the carburetor on his 1953 Ford F100 was leaking.

And Then Riley Said . . .

"There's more West on Mars than there is in Utah."

Familiar with Riley's unique turn of mind, no one attempted to challenge his statement.

A Curve in the Road

How stupid can you get setting out across the frozen Canadian tundra on your own to prove a hair-brained point? Craig chided himself. He'd told his drinking buddies at the Smokin Gun he could walk between Waskada, where he lived, and Melita, Manitoba, some 23 miles to the northwest, in six hours. Money was put on the bar and a wager was set. It was January and temperatures between the two provincial hamlets routinely dropped into the minus-zero category, even during daylight. He'd imposed dimwit challenges on himself before—some pretty nuts—but this one could kill him, especially since he'd be taking the so-called "as the crows fly" route far off the main road and any sign of civilization. "Every damn time you get sloshed you make dumb bets," he mumbled angrily. He'd been hiking two hours but wasn't really sure how far he'd traveled—hangovers did not enhance his cognitive abilities. *Probably a half-dozen miles. Shit, three times that to go,* he estimated. Already feeling exhausted, he stooped to catch his breath. It was then he caught site of a Burma Shave sign. "Huh, out here? What the hell!" he blurted. When he couldn't see another one in any direction, he knew he was in deep trouble.

A Moving Experience

Never confuse motion with action.
—Benjamin Franklin

For 30-years, Walt had driven a semi on the backroads of the west hauling petroleum equipment to remote sites. It was something that gave him pleasure, because he loved rolling through the majestic hinterlands of the region. In all, it was a satisfying way to make a paycheck, and he'd managed to bank quite a bundle. When he took early retirement, he decided to buy a place in the area he'd been traveling for so many years. *Be nice just to settle in the foothills of the Salt River Range or Big Horn Mountains,* he thought, and he did just that. One-hundred-forty-eight acres and a two-bedroom cabin were his for a price he could well afford. However, it wasn't long after he moved in he became restless and went back to work, concluding things just didn't look quite as good when they stood still.

Fate Can Be a Bastard

It was on the loneliest stretch of the high-plains in eastern Montana that Larry's car broke down. There he sat in his 12-year-old Chevy Silverado looking out of its windows and rearview mirrors hoping to see a car that might come to his aid. But hours came and went and he began to worry that he might have to spend the night where he was. He knew from the map that there was no town for dozens of miles, so walking was out of the question. Now as the sun began to set, he worried that the temperature might go below zero, even though it was late April. *I'll freeze to death out here unless someone comes along and stops,* he told himself. As things turned out, that's exactly what happened . . . no one came along.

Life Fulfilled

What really upset him about dying was leaving the open road and his beloved camper van. He'd made a wonderful life for himself the last few years, and he was thankful for the joy he'd experienced traveling and meeting new people. Now, as he faced his final sunset, he thanked his maker for allowing him to reach Wakeeney, Kansas.

Girl Falls into Canyon

She paces, now and again looking up at the dark clouds.
—David Romtvedt

Gloria was going to come back and devote herself to painting the Horseshoe Bend overlook when she grew up and became an artist. There was no one she admired more than Georgia O'Keeffe, and she dreamed of doing for Arizona what her idol had done for New Mexico. In three years, she'd be going to art school, and then she'd move to the Glen Canyon National Recreational area and start her life's work. She had it all figured out and it excited her beyond words. Her parents brought her to the site as often as they could and cherished her sketches of the wilderness, recognizing in her a true talent for capturing the raw beauty of the desert gorge. After their daughter accidentally fell from the crest of the 700 foot-peak, they could no longer abide the sight of her drawings, cursing the first time they decided to take her to the park rather than Disneyland.

Mama Said It Was His Special Place, but We Never Knew Why

At least twice a year, Daddy would take my baby sister and me on a Sunday ride to Tryon. It was an hour drive from our house in North Platte, and along the way we'd stop for a picnic lunch in a field with a big Cottonwood tree. As soon as we got to Tryon, Daddy would turn the car around and we'd head home. We didn't mind going there so many times, but when we got a little older we asked why he always took us to the same place. "Cuz . . ."' he answered.

Roadblocks

For most of his adult life Dan had the notion he might one day buy a small piece of property—a spread, as they called it out there on the eastern plains of Colorado. As a kid he'd accompanied his father on business trips from St. Paul to Salt Lake City a couple of times and had fallen under the spell of that part of the country. It spoke to him for reasons he could not quite articulate. All he knew it was a place he wanted to be. Now, at 65, recently retired and widowed, he figured it was the perfect time to follow his instincts. To go to his "happy place," as he'd long thought of it. So, he packed up his house, sold off everything, including the house itself, and prepared to head west. He was excited by the prospect of what may await him in the wide-open spaces. It seemed the first time he was going to have an actual adventure. And then a thought seized him as he climbed into his car. *It's probably going to be lonely as hell out there.*

Armed and Dangerous?

There's a fast draw competition in the court yard of the Virginian Hotel in Medicine Bow. We don't know it's a contest and think there's a real shootout going on, so we quickly drive away. When we reach the next town on Route 287, we're told it's an annual event and one worth seeing. Should we make the trek back, we ask ourselves, but decide we were lucky to get out of there alive and continue on our way to Rawlins.

Encounter at Fourmile

Where there's smoke there's . . .
—Proverb

While tidying up the old cabin on her northern Wyoming ranch in advance of visitors, Dollie detected something burning. When she peered out of a back window, she saw smoke and flames a hundred yards away. *Must be one of the energy company's transformers*, she surmised. For the past decade, she'd leased the mineral rights to her property and this was the first time she'd had a problem, aside from having to report a light at a compressor station was interfering with her star gazing. After a call to the company's field manager, the errant illumination was quickly doused. It had been that kind of a trouble-free partnership with an enterprise that was putting good money in her pocket, something that had been needed since the sheep ranching operation came to an end because her husband had taken ill and had to retire. Moreover, she was getting on in years herself and didn't feel up to running it. Dollie quickly made an emergency call and within minutes energy workers were putting out the flames. Moments after they'd arrived on the scene, a helicopter dropped a load of slurry which finished off the fire. What remained was a charred depression an acre wide. Always a woman of sound enterprise and keen imagination, she put the event to good use by regaling her tourist guests with a story about how an unidentified flying object had almost hit her. Until the winter and spring snow and rain had restored the natural ground cover, she had convincing evidence that something of an alien nature had attempted contact.

Why They Moved Away

At the center of the dried creek bed stood the towering remains of a Utah Juniper. It looked like the arm and hand of a skeleton. Regardless of the time of day, the shadow it cast remained fixed on the farmhouse and barn that had once been the homestead of the Redding family. It was only when the wind blew hard and caused the fingers of the ghostly silhouette to tremble that one could discern a slight moan.

"You Got Yourself Some Kind of Imagination, Son!"

On the far western horizon, a dust devil reached high into the noonday sky. A common late summer event on the Willoughby's 6,000-acre ranch in southeastern Montana. Travis seldom paid attention to the mini-cyclones, but he thought this one was different than the rest. "Paw, look at that, will you," he uttered to the elderly figure in the rocker next to him. "Well, I'll be danged. Ain't never seen one like that, for sure," replied the wizened rancher gazing in the direction his son pointed. "Maybe it's one of them weird thingies been flyin' round here lately," observed Travis. "Now, there you go again, boy. Just because its lifting up cattle with its purple talons don't mean it's some kind of space creature."

Wind Instrument

The ridge that loomed over the Iverson's cabin on their 20,000-acre sheep ranch in northern Wyoming was called Symphony Rock. Depending on the velocity of the gusts, various melodies—all rooted in music of the Baroque tradition—emanated from it. This occasioned the departure of all three Iverson children when each turned 18 because of their desire for a more contemporary playlist.

Adjusting to One's Surroundings

Rattlesnakes were everywhere on the mesa, and she was terrified of running into one. She moved cautiously along the narrow dirt path that spanned the historic Fetterman battleground and every couple of steps she stamped her feet because she'd heard that the noise and vibrations would scare the reptiles into hiding. When she got back to her friend's house where she was staying for the week, she was told that if you got near a rattler and stomped the ground it would likely strike at you out of fear it was being attacked. From that point on, she would only venture into the wilds when there were tires under her.

Fear on a Very Large Scale

Jessie loved to drive into the high plains late afternoons and sit on the hood of his pickup and watch the sun slip over the infinite horizon. He liked how the light would flatten out in the last seconds before it was gone as if clinging to the Earth's curve might delay the approaching darkness. He wondered if night was also the Sun's boogieman.

ABOUT THE AUTHOR

Michael C. Keith is the author of 15 story collections and an acclaimed memoir *(The Next Better Place)*. He retired emeritus professor in the Communication Department at Boston College. Prior to his four decades in academe, Keith was a radio broadcaster. He has been nominated for several awards for his fiction and is the recipient of numerous accolades for his books on media subjects.

www.ingramcontent.com/pod-product-compliance
Lightning Source LLC
LaVergne TN
LVHW050950080826
845145LV00004B/1457

* 9 7 8 1 9 5 0 0 6 3 2 8 4 *